CW00689848

FAITH
UNDERSTANDING

Vital Lessons from Psalm 73

*But when I thought how to understand this, it seemed to
me a wearisome task, until I went into the sanctuary of
God; then I discerned their end.*
Psalm 73:16-17

Iain D. Campbell

THE BANNER OF TRUTH TRUST

THE BANNER OF TRUTH TRUST
3 Murrayfield Road, Edinburgh EH12 6EL, UK
PO Box 621, Carlisle, PA 17013, USA

*

© The Banner of Truth Trust 2015

ISBN:
Print: 978 1 84871 533 2
EPUB: 978 1 84871 534 9
Kindle: 978 1 84871 535 6

*

Typeset in 11/15 pt Adobe Garamond Pro at
The Banner of Truth Trust, Edinburgh

Printed in the USA by
Versa Press, Inc.,
East Peoria, IL.

*

FAITH SEEKING
UNDERSTANDING

But when I thought how to understand this,
it seemed to me a wearisome task,
until I went into the sanctuary of God;
then I discerned their end.—Psalm 73:16-17

IF you are a regular reader of the Bible, you will know that the *Book of Psalms* is a remarkable book. It has many unique and outstanding features. It is, after all, the longest of the books in the collection that we know as the Bible. In it we have the longest and the shortest chapter in the Bible. We have multiple authorship and we have the largest collection of prophecies and predictions gathered together in any Old Testament book. If you add up all the Old Testament quotations in the New Testament you will discover that the quotations from the *Book of Psalms* outnumber the quotations from any other book of the Old Testament.

This book also brings together the great themes of the Bible. It speaks about God—Father, Son, and Holy Spirit; it speaks about the flow of redemptive history, as it celebrates creation, providence, redemption, incarnation, Christ's reign, and return; it speaks about personal salvation, as it highlights the themes of guilt, cleansing, obedience, holiness, desire, prayer, security, doubt, and assurance; and it speaks of the church, as it reminds us that God's people are his flock, his priesthood, his kingdom, and his family.

Martin Luther was therefore quite justified when he described the *Book of Psalms* as 'a little Bible'.[1] I think one of the things he meant by that was that all the great issues of the Bible intersect and meet and are expressed in one way or another in the *Book of Psalms*. It is a compilation of holy songs which look backwards, forwards, upwards and inwards. King David, who wrote many of the Psalms, is described as 'the sweet psalmist of Israel' (*2 Sam.* 23:1), who spoke as a prophet from God (*Acts* 2:30).

But I also like John Calvin's approach to the *Book of Psalms*. In the preface to his commentary on the Psalms, Calvin tells us about his view of the Psalter:

> I have been accustomed to call this book, I think not inappropriately, 'An Anatomy of all the Parts of the Soul'; for there is not an emotion of which anyone can be conscious that is not here represented as in a mirror. Or rather, the Holy Spirit has here drawn to the life all the griefs, sorrows, fears, doubts, hopes, cares, perplexities, in short, all the distracting emotions with which the minds of men are wont to be agitated.[2]

'An Anatomy of all the Parts of the Soul' is a magnificent description of the Psalms. When you know that something is wrong in your body, you want to go to somebody who knows

[1] Luther says of the *Book of Psalms* that 'it might well be entitled a Little Bible, wherein everything contained in the entire Bible is beautifully and briefly comprehended…' (Preface to the German Psalter 1531, quoted online at http://www.cprf.co.uk/quotes/martinlutherpsalter.htm, accessed 7 September 2013).

[2] John Calvin, *Commentary on the Book of Psalms*, vol. 1, (Edinburgh: Calvin Translation Society, 1845), pp. xxxvi-vii.

anatomy. Some organ, internal or external, is malfunctioning and not doing what it is designed to do; there is unexplained pain somewhere where there should not be: these sensations tell you that something is wrong, and it requires treatment. So you want an expert on the human body to deal with the situation. You want somebody who knows all about the body, who knows all about the different bits that make up the body, which bits you can do without, which bits can be taken away without you dropping dead on the spot, which bits can be replaced, and which bits work in conjunction with which other bits. Before you subject your body to any kind of medical inspection or procedure, you want to make sure the person who is treating you has studied the subject and knows all about it.

But where will you go when your *soul* begins to malfunction? Where will you go when pain registers in the non-physical 'bits' of you that no surgeon can dissect and no doctor can remove or prod or measure or replace? There are parts to you that cannot be put on a table and operated on or put in a box and buried; bits that cannot be measured, weighed, or removed—there are feelings, longings, desires, wishes, dreams, regrets, and memories; things that are non-physical and invisible, yet at one level are the *real* you. When these begin to malfunction and when pain registers in one of these elements, where will you go? Where is the expert in the anatomy of the soul to whom you can go when your soul requires urgent medical attention?

Calvin's suggestion is that you could do no better than go to this ancient Hebrew hymnbook that God gave to his people many, many years ago. Here, says Calvin, 'the heart is brought into the light'. In this collection there are psalms, hymns, and spiritual songs that arose out of the experience of some of the psalmists. They convey the psalmists' delight in the things of God and in the ways and works of God, which God gave to his people to be liturgised and to be the fabric of their worship; there is a remarkable insight into the nature of Christian experience, in all its ups and downs. Come to this *Book of Psalms* if you want an anatomy of the parts of your soul. Come with me to Psalm 73; it is the classic case of a Psalm that deals powerfully with a malfunctioning soul. Out of this particular psalm-writer's experience comes one of the most honest, and most moving passages in the Bible. In it, a man of faith is faced with a problem he cannot resolve. He wants to understand it, but he does not, and cannot understand it until he comes into God's sanctuary. Let us join him there, as our faith seeks understanding too.

1. The problem Asaph could not resolve

Psalm 73 tells us that there was an issue which Asaph, who wrote this psalm, could not work out. He tried to, but he failed. What was the situation which he tells us was painful for him? What was wrong with his soul? There were some elements that fed into his pain.

First, there was the doctrine which he professed

Asaph, the author of this psalm which stands at the head of the third book of the Psalter, was brought up on good Old Testament covenant theology (not that I think that there is bad Old Testament covenant theology, but it is possible to learn Old Testament covenant theology badly). Asaph had been taught the best covenant theology well. It had been in his ears from the earliest days as a child member of God's covenant community. From the moment he had heard anything at all, he had heard about God's goodness to Israel, the covenant love that had led to God's special relationship to the people whom he had chosen to be a light to the nations. God so loved the world that he chose Israel and he placed in Israel the light of the gospel that was to extend into all the world.

In an act of sheer sovereign grace God called Abraham—just another Mesopotamian idol-worshipper—and gave him grace to trust and obey him. God had said to Abraham, 'I will make you a blessing and all the nations of the world will be blessed in you' (see *Gen.* 12:2-3). By way of fulfilling that promise, God bound himself in covenant to the sons of Abraham, to Isaac and Jacob (whom he later called Israel). The sons of Jacob through Judah (the Jews) became the bearers of God's truth to the world, and at last, Jesus was born from that line. God was good to Israel: 'to them', says Paul, 'belonged the glories, and the covenants, the giving of the law, and the promises, and the Messiah' (see *Rom.* 9:4-5).

But Asaph also knew that the blessing of God's salvation was not simply a matter of ethnicity. God was good to Israel; on the stage of human history he chose one human family to be a means of blessing to the whole world. But the blessing—then as now—was to those 'who are pure in heart' (*Psa.* 73:1). Asaph knew this too; he knew that what God requires of us is not just to come with the sacrifices which he appoints, or to make sure that we have the liturgy right. God requires a clean heart. Consider the following passages:

… if they confess their iniquity … if then their uncircumcised heart is humbled and they make amends for their iniquity, then I will remember my covenant with Jacob, and I will remember my covenant with Isaac and my covenant with Abraham, and I will remember the land' (*Lev.* 26:40-42).

Hear, O Israel: The Lord our God, the Lord is one. You shall love the Lord your God with all your heart and with all your soul and with all your might. And these words that I command you today shall be on your heart (*Deut.* 6:4-6).

Yet the Lord set his heart in love on your fathers and chose their offspring after them, you above all peoples, as you are this day. Circumcise therefore the foreskin of your heart, and be no longer stubborn (*Deut.* 10:15-16).

For you will not delight in sacrifice, or I would give it; you will not be pleased with a burnt offering. The sacrifices of God are a broken spirit; a broken and contrite heart, O God, you will not despise (*Psa.* 51:16-17).

These are interesting passages, and they take us to the heart of Asaph's religion. God required circumcision—yet physical circumcision was not enough if a man's heart was not 'circumcised'. He demanded sacrifices; yet sacrifices meant nothing if a man's heart was not clean. Jesus preached the same message. It is the 'pure in heart', he said, that will see God (*Matt.* 5:8). The 'heart' of the new covenant was the promise of a new heart:

But this is the covenant that I will make with the house of Israel after those days, declares the Lord: I will put my law within them, and I will write it on their hearts. And I will be their God, and they shall be my people (*Jer.* 31:33).

All the mechanisms for Israel's religion—law, temple, sacrifice, prophets, and priests—were to bring this lesson before the people: God's grace reached Israel to convey the truth that Asaph believed: 'God is good to Israel, to those who are pure in heart.'

Second, there was the experience he encountered

But for Asaph, there was a day, maybe more than one, when he looked around and suddenly said, 'Every day of my life I am seeing my God defied, denied and rejected by a world that doesn't want to know him; I'm seeing people acting in violence and pride and arrogance, people who set their mouths against heaven and blaspheme God, people who reject him and say, "We don't want this God to reign over us."'

And these were the people who seemed to be getting on! These were the people to whom God in his goodness and benevolence seemed to be giving so much. 'They have more than their hearts could wish', says Asaph. 'They are not in trouble like other men.' Asaph saw them living in a wicked way, without any sense of sin or repentance, in denial and rejection of God, their hearts and minds and consciences closed to the invitations of God's grace—yet God was good to them!

Materially, they had everything. Morally, they wore pride like a garment and violence like a robe. God was not in their thoughts at all. Asaph saw them—neighbours, colleagues, friends, enemies—he observed them living in sin and wickedness, and God seemed to be good to them. And as for himself, well—he was simply trying to do what God wanted him to do: he was 'washing his hands' and keeping his heart clean. He was trying to live the life that God wanted him to live, according to the requirements of the covenant, and it was getting him nowhere. Asaph was doing his utmost to please God and to walk humbly before him, yet he concludes that it's all been in vain. He cannot match his theology with his experience. He believes in the promises of God and yet what he is seeing all around him seems to belie these very promises. The promise said: 'God is good to those who seek him and who walk humbly before him.' Asaph said: 'I am seeking God and seeking to walk humbly before him.' Yet apparently God was much better to those who did *not* seek him, and walked in pride and arrogance.

For Asaph, experience seemed to clash with theology. His covenant theology said one thing; yet it seemed to be contradicted by what he saw with his eyes every day. God seems to be good to the wicked and his own people were struggling and burdened, confused and alone.

I don't know if you have stood in Asaph's place. Have you tried to maintain all the disciplines that you know are fitting and right for a healthy Christian life and sometimes found that it's getting you nowhere? You have few material possessions compared with others. You struggle in your work and with your family, while next door and down the street and across the road are people who never go to church or read their Bible, who mock the things of God and who seem to be trouble-free. As far as you can see, God is very good to them.

Asaph was in that place, and he found it to be a place from which he could so easily fall to the ground helpless: 'God is good to Israel', he said, 'to those who are pure in heart. But as for me, my feet had almost stumbled' (*Psa.* 73:1-2). Indeed, Asaph confesses that he was jealous of the wicked! He envied them their

God-free life! I have heard many testimonies of people who were converted by God's grace and who said, 'Well, I came to the point when I knew I wasn't a Christian and I envied what Christians had.' But here is a place in the Bible where the testimony is the very reverse of that. It is one thing for an unbeliever to envy the peace of the Christian; but it is something else for the Christian to envy the peace of the wicked! I have never heard that testimony in a church. I have never heard a Christian stand up and say that he wished he had what his unconverted neighbours have. Have you?

But I tell you, I am glad this psalm is here; and I am as amazed at the honesty of this believer as I am humbled at the provision God makes for his people by inserting a psalm like this in the Psalter. There was a very interesting article about Psalm singing written some time ago by Dr Carl Trueman, in which he asked, 'What can miserable Christians sing?'[3] It is an important and profound question. So much of what is sung in contemporary church life is not for miserable Christians. The assumption behind many of the songs that are sung in Christian worship today is that Christians are never miserable! But sometimes they are, as Asaph was. And when you are a miserable Christian, here is a song you can sing.

In this psalm he confesses something else too; he says that the thoughts he was harbouring, the jealousies he was feeling towards those who were strangers to God and his grace, were things he could not tell any of his brothers or sisters. I actually think that is a remarkable spark of grace in the midst of the darkness. 'If I had said "I will speak thus," I would have betrayed the generation

[3] C. R. Trueman, *The Wages of Spin: Critical Writings on Historical and Contemporary Evangelicalism* (Fearn, Ross-shire: Christian Focus, 2004), pp. 158-60.

of your children' (*Psa.* 73:15). I think the idea there is, 'I didn't want to share this with anyone in case my feelings would cause someone else to stumble.' When you have a problem in the Christian life it is good to be able to share it, to have a Christian friend with whom you can speak about it. But sometimes there are things that you cannot share. For Asaph, these thoughts were not for sharing simply because he did not want any of his brothers or sisters to stumble. That's good. That shows that his concern was for God, even though he could not figure out God's ways with him.

So Asaph tries to rationalise his situation in life, and it is beyond his capacity to work it out. It causes him grief and pain, and he is in darkness. Until, that is, he went 'into the sanctuary of God' (*Psa.* 73:17). Let's think about that for a moment.

2. The place to which Asaph came

Now it is not that Asaph had not been in the sanctuary of God before. In many ways that was part of the problem. He was no stranger to the sanctuary. To have seen Asaph coming and going from the sanctuary you would never have imagined what was going on in his heart. Do you not feel like that sometimes? Aren't you glad that people don't know what you are really feeling when they see you at church?

But that is where Asaph went—into the sanctuary, and he says, '*then* I understood'. These simple words express a fundamental and intimate connection between the sanctuary of God on the one hand, and the understanding of Asaph on the other. Reason had given no understanding to Asaph's faith, but the sanctuary did. What reason could not do, a meeting with God did. There was a point where Asaph's reason had to give way to God's revelation. Only then did Asaph understand.

What was the sanctuary?

Several of the psalms at this point in the Psalter have to do with the 'sanctuary', with God's holy place. That was what the sanctuary was for Asaph: God's holy place. The history of the sanctuary begins with Moses: God had said to Moses 'make me a sanctuary' (*Exod.* 25:8). The word 'sanctuary' means a 'holy place', holy because God would dwell there.

That does not mean, of course, that God needs a place in which to live. As Paul said, preaching in the Greek city of Athens, 'The God who made the world and everything in it, being Lord of heaven and earth, does not live in temples made by man' (*Acts* 17:24). Yet in his grace and mercy he came to 'dwell' among his people, so as to become accessible to them.

The tabernacle, the place in which God would dwell, was a special tent, which Moses had to build in a special way, and for a special purpose. It would travel with the Israelites in their wilderness journey until they came to the promised land. And it was the place where God's presence lived among them. None of them could say that God didn't know what it was like to be a pilgrim; they were pilgrims with him (see *Psa.* 39:12).

God had brought his people to Sinai, where he had revealed his glory and given them his law. But they could not come near that mountain. God's presence would consume them; his glory would be their death! Yet God provided a way for that glory to live among them. His presence would be with them to comfort them, not to consume them, to lead and guide them, not to destroy them. And where this tent went, they went.

Yet this was only temporary. One of the first things God had promised to give Abraham was a land for his descendants (*Gen.* 12:1). That promise was reiterated to the Israelites when God took them out of the land of Egypt (*Exod.* 6:8). So when the Israelites came into the promised land, God gave them a permanent sanctuary. He promised David that Solomon, his son, would be the builder of the temple, which God describes as 'a house for my name' (*2 Sam.* 7:13). David's charge to Solomon made this explicit: '… the LORD has chosen you to build a house for the sanctuary' (*1 Chron.* 28:10). The temple replaced the tabernacle. God would dwell in Jerusalem, the city of David.

Solomon's prayer at the dedication of the temple gives a marvellous description of the nature and purpose of the sanctuary:

> But will God indeed dwell on the earth? Behold, heaven and the highest heaven cannot contain you; how much less this house that I have built! Yet have regard to the prayer of your servant and to his plea, O LORD my God, listening to the cry and to the prayer that your servant prays before you this day, that your eyes may be open night and day towards this house, the place of which you have said, 'My name shall be there,' that you may listen to the prayer that your servant offers towards this place. And listen to the plea of your servant and of your people Israel, when they pray towards this place. And listen in heaven your dwelling place, and when you hear, forgive (*1 Kings* 8:27-30).

This is why the sanctuary was so important. It was God's dwelling place, the place of disclosure and revelation, the place where God made himself known to his people. Again and again the psalms delight that such a place exists for the people of God:

Hear the voice of my pleas for mercy, when I cry to you for help, when I lift up my hands towards your most holy sanctuary (*Psa.* 28:2).

I have looked upon you in the sanctuary, beholding your power and glory (*Psa.* 63:2).

Praise the LORD! Praise God in his sanctuary; praise him in his mighty heavens! (*Psa.* 150:1).

And it is why the psalmist could delight to join God's people when they said to him, 'Let us go to the house of the LORD!' (*Psa.* 122:1).

That was Asaph's delight too. He was often in the sanctuary, worshipping God in his temple. And now, in Psalm 73, he says that the sanctuary became for him the place of disclosure, where he finally understood; he could now make sense of the issues that had been plaguing him and leaving him feeling miserable. For Asaph there is a great connection between the place where God makes himself known and the insight that he, as a believer, needed. What a remarkable condescension on God's part, that he should not only establish a dwelling place for himself in tabernacle and temple, and give a whole set of detailed instructions to his people about how he is to be worshipped, but that he also intended to help them in their pilgrimage by means of that same sanctuary.

In commenting on this psalm, and on these words in particular, John Calvin says, 'until God become my schoolmaster, and until I learn by his word what otherwise my mind cannot comprehend, I understand nothing.'[4] Until God becomes our schoolmaster and

[4] *Commentary on the Book of Psalms,* vol. 3, (Edinburgh: Calvin Translation Society, 1847), p. 142.

we come to the place where God makes himself known and reveals himself and opens his mind to us, we will understand nothing; nothing about him, his world, or our own experience in it. The theatre of God's glory becomes our classroom.

Where is our sanctuary?

So where is our sanctuary? Do we have to go to Jerusalem? Do we need to make a pilgrimage to a holy site in order to meet with God? Is there a holy land where God makes himself known? No! In fact, God has given us a better and more glorious sanctuary than God's people ever had in Jerusalem. Someone stands before us in the gospel and says 'I tell you, something greater than the temple is here' (*Matt.* 12:6). That 'something' is Jesus.

It is not necessary for us to travel to Jerusalem, but it is still possible for us to come into God's sanctuary. In Jesus, the presence of God came down to earth; Jesus was a real man, but he was the eternal Son of God. This is how the Apostle John, who begins his Gospel by calling Jesus the 'Word' who was in the beginning with God, describes his presence among men: 'the Word became flesh and dwelt among us, and we have seen his glory, glory as of the only Son from the Father, full of grace and truth' (*John* 1:14). The word 'dwelt' comes from the word meaning a tent; Jesus, the eternal Son of God pitched his tent, or 'tabernacled' among us. John says that he saw the glory of Jesus; it dwelt among men in Jesus, just as it had dwelt in the tabernacle and the temple long ago.

But we know that Jesus is no longer on earth; he has returned to the throne of heaven. Yet he is with us still, in the person and by the work of the Holy Spirit. The Father who sends Jesus, his

Son, to the world, now, in and along with Jesus, sends the Spirit to us. And where the Holy Spirit is, Jesus is; Paul reminds us that 'the Lord is the Spirit' (*2 Cor.* 3:17). The presence of the Holy Spirit with us is the presence of Jesus with us. For that reason, the New Testament can say that 'we are the temple of the living God; as God said, "I will make my dwelling among them and walk among them, and I will be their God, and they shall be my people"' (*2 Cor.* 6:16).

But that is not all; for Jesus promised that 'where two or three are gathered in my name, there am I among them' (*Matt.* 18:20). Where is our sanctuary? Where is the presence of God known? Where does God reveal himself to us? He reveals himself in the place where his word is proclaimed and where his people gather for worship. In the place of such worshipping people, Paul says, it is possible that an unbeliever may enter and 'worship God and declare that God is really among you' (*1 Cor.* 14:25). That is why Paul can write about his calling to be a minister of the gospel in the elevated language of Ephesians 3:7-12:

> Of this gospel I was made a minister according to the gift of God's grace, which was given me by the working of his power. To me, though I am the very least of all the saints, this grace was given, to preach to the Gentiles the unsearchable riches of Christ, and to bring to light for everyone what is the plan of the mystery hidden for ages in God who created all things, so that through the church the manifold wisdom of God might now be made known to the rulers and authorities in the heavenly places. This was according to the eternal purpose that he has realized in Christ Jesus our Lord, in whom we have boldness and access with confidence through our faith in him.

He concludes the chapter with a prayer that God would have 'glory in the church' forever (*Eph.* 3:21).

So our sanctuary is wherever Jesus meets with us by his Spirit, through his word. For Asaph, the holy place of God's revelation was in the Jerusalem temple, but now God has tabernacled among us, and dwells among us in a more glorious and unique way. He reveals his will by the preaching of his word. The God who now in the gospel of redeeming grace makes himself known to us through Jesus Christ by his word through his Spirit is our sanctuary.

The connection between the sanctuary and the understanding that we all need still exists. We need to come back to God's word, read and preached, time and again. Until God becomes our schoolmaster and we submit our minds to the authority of God's word, we will understand nothing. The great Baptist preacher, C. H. Spurgeon, comments on this psalm and says of Asaph that 'his mind entered the eternity where God dwells as in a holy place. He left the things of sense for the things invisible. His heart gazed within the veil. He stood where the thrice-holy God stands.'[5]

What do you expect when you come to your church for worship on the Lord's day? Part of the tragedy of contemporary evangelicalism is that the church is so much a carbon copy of the culture around us that people come into it and get only what they have been getting every other day of the week. As a minister of the gospel I don't want my people to get *that* when they come for worship. I want them to enter the eternity where God dwells.

[5] C. H. Spurgeon, *The Treasury of David*, vol. 2 (Peabody, Mass.: Hendrickson, 1988), pp. 250-51.

I want them to cross the threshold of church on the Lord's day and get a glimpse of eternity, not because I think there is some mystical presence in a building which has been consecrated for holy service, but because the preaching of the word is the way God makes himself known. Whether you are in a church building or not, you can be in the sanctuary of God. Around God's word, worshipping him and listening together to his voice in the fellowship of his people, men and women enter into the eternity where God dwells. They are able then to gaze on things that are invisible. They can rise above the things of time to the things of eternity, above the mundane to the heavenly, above the temporary to the permanent.

Isn't that how Paul tells us to live a solid and a healthy Christian life? The important thing is to 'look not to the things that are seen but to the things that are unseen. For the things that are seen are transient, but the things that are unseen are eternal' (*2 Cor.* 4:18). There is much more to be seen than can be seen with the eyes. There are some things that can only be seen with the heart.

Asaph's experience tells me that a believer's soul begins to malfunction when he confines his reason to what his eyes can see. When you do that it is painful. But when you come into God's sanctuary and listen to God's voice, when you engage with God's word and you let God be your schoolmaster, then your heart will see more than your eyes can see.

Do you remember that moment in the book of Genesis when Joseph brought his sons to Jacob for a blessing? Jacob was old and blind; 'the eyes of Israel were dim with age, so that he could not see' (*Gen.* 48:10). Joseph helped him in the act of blessing by placing his firstborn son, Manasseh, under Jacob's right hand;

that's what reason told him to do. But Jacob crossed his hands, so that the right hand of blessing was on the younger son, Ephraim. Joseph was not happy and tried to right the wrong; but Jacob had crossed his hands purposefully: he had been in God's sanctuary. The blind man could see further than any. Jacob saw with his heart into God's purposes; we must do the same.

3. The perspective Asaph gained

There were things that Asaph could not know and would not know until he came into the sanctuary of God and God became his schoolmaster. That is where faith receives understanding. What, then, were those things that Asaph learned from God's word in God's house? What did Asaph discover in God's sanctuary that he could not have known otherwise? In God's sanctuary, Asaph was reminded of three great realities.

(1) The sovereignty of God's throne

Asaph was reminded, first of all, that there is absolutely nothing that happens in the course of this world's history, or in our lives, apart from the absolute rule, plan, and permission of God. Listen to what Asaph says:

> '… when I thought how to understand this, it seemed to me a wearisome task, until I went into the sanctuary of God; then I discerned their end. Truly you set them in slippery places …' (*Psa.* 73:16-18).

That's the first thing: '*You* set them …' Asaph had to be reminded of the most basic lesson of all—that these wicked people he envied had not set themselves anywhere. It was God who was in control of their lives. So much of the first part of the psalm was about Asaph himself; but in the sanctuary he was reminded that it is actually all about God. It is God's throne that rules all. Just for a moment Asaph had forgotten that there is a throne above every other throne, and on it reigns the God who holds the past, the present, and the future, so that every atom of every life, and every part of every experience, are subject to the sovereignty and absolute dominion that belong to the Lord alone.

It is not the wicked who are in charge; they may flourish and prosper, rising to great ranks of honour and preferment; they may have 'everything', but that everything is subject to the lordship of God. When Asaph came into the sanctuary of God, his mind was raised above the phenomena that had caused him so much heartache and grief, and he saw the sovereign throne of God.

Do you remember that moment in the book of Revelation when the Apostle John experienced the same thing? There he was, banished to the small Aegean island of Patmos because of the ascendant sovereignty of the Roman empire, having outlived the other disciples and now alone with memories of better days and the prospect of a bleak future.

Yet he had been keeping his Lord's day holy, as best he could, with worship and meditation, and one special Lord's day he was 'in the Spirit' (*Rev.* 1:10). A voice spoke, and things were shown to him (that's why it was a *Revelation*) that he could otherwise never have seen. John had a door opened for him in heaven (*Rev.* 4:1), and through it he saw a throne! The ultimate power in the universe belonged not to Rome or to Caesar, but to God and to his Christ!

That is not something you see easily if you confine your thoughts to what you see of your neighbour's lifestyle, or what you see on your television screen. But you do see it in God's presence in his sanctuary, as Jesus, by his word and Spirit, reveals himself to his people.

In that sanctuary, you see the Governor of the universe—one God, Father, Son and Holy Spirit—governing with infinite and unbounded sovereignty over all things. Your heart can see it with the eyes of faith, as faith is led and instructed by the word of God. This is the unadulterated teaching of Scripture from beginning to end: 'in the beginning,' says Genesis 1, 'God created the heavens and the earth.' Where did this magnificent universe of ours come from? It came from a point of origin in the mind and purpose of the God who was there before the beginning began.

In the beginning the Word already was, and the triune God, in the infinite and unchangeable glory of his magnificent eternal being and independence, purposed to create a universe. In that work of creation he is absolutely sovereign. He has no help in it; there is nothing in energy or in particles that causes a big explosion to result in an ordered universe seasoned by months and years, complete with planets in perfect orbit. God did it, sovereign over creation.

But he is also sovereign over the events that take place in his creation. Once he made it he didn't walk away from it. I observe wind, earthquake, and fire; I see the changes of the seasons; I see the events of everyday life—all this I see with my eyes; but I come into the sanctuary of God and I see it with my heart. He is the one that sends out the rain and the wind and the hail and the snow to do his bidding because he is the absolute sovereign over all things.

And what about the difficult circumstances of which Asaph speaks? They are all under the providence of God. Richard Sibbes, the great Puritan, has a wonderful sermon on this psalm. 'This entering into God's sanctuary,' says Sibbes, 'is the way to free us from dangerous scandals and overcome dangerous conflicts.' And he goes on to say,

> For the conclusions of the sanctuary are clean contrary to the conclusions of sensible[6] carnal reason. Carnal reason says, is there any providence that rules in the earth, is there a God in heaven that suffers these things to go so confusedly? Aye, but the word of God in the sanctuary says there is a providence that rules all things sweetly.[7]

Perhaps you may have been tempted to ask in your darker moments, 'Can there be a God in heaven that suffers these things to go so confusedly?' Come into the sanctuary with Asaph, and there let your heart see the God who in his providence rules all things sweetly.

In the sanctuary you will also see him sovereign in salvation, in electing, in calling, in justifying, in adopting, in glorifying his people—he has it all in his hands. Were it otherwise, how could any of us preach at all? In preaching the gospel we are calling sinners who are dead in trespasses and sins to come out of their graves and to live new lives in Christ Jesus! It is an impossibility until we remember that God is sovereign in salvation too, and from him 'new life the dead receive'.

Come into the sanctuary and you will see the sovereignty of the God who has determined that all of those sinners he ever promised to give to his Son will come to him, and those who

[6] *i.e.*, dependent on the senses.

[7] Richard Sibbes, 'The Saint's Resolution', in *Works of Richard Sibbes,* Vol. 7 (Edinburgh: Banner of Truth Trust, 2001), p. 83.

will come to him he will in no wise cast out. Asaph saw that: he caught a vision of the absolute sovereignty of God.

(2) The silencing of God's enemies

And then when Asaph came into the sanctuary he understood this too, he understood that the place on which those rebellious, wilfully rebellious, sinners were standing was a slippery place. He thought *he* was the one falling; and sometimes believers do stumble and fall, but they always fall into everlasting arms. But sinners, on the other hand, have no security whatsoever. In the sanctuary of God Asaph understood their end. He realised that all their possessions in this world could be lost in a moment and then they have nothing. 'Without warning, without escape and without hope,' says Spurgeon, 'you set them in slippery places.'

Asaph had forgotten that. He was envious of what sinners have, but when he came into the sanctuary he realised just how slender the thread is that holds them. The God who gives wealth can take it away in an instant. Riches are like a dream, like a mirage. Jesus says, 'lay up for yourselves treasures in heaven, where neither moth nor rust destroys and where thieves do not break in and steal' (*Matt.* 6:20). Everything here is subject to rust and decay and theft. Sinners stand in slippery places.

In fact, one of the great questions that Psalm 73 forces you to ask is—Where are you standing? What is the foundation of your life? Is Jesus Christ your solid rock? Or are you resting on the things of this world? Only one thing matters, and that is to have Jesus as Lord and Saviour. God will silence his enemies and defend his friends. Are you his friend?

(3) The security of God's people

Asaph was God's friend, even though he confesses to being envious of God's enemies. But in the sanctuary he learned afresh that God was in control, that his enemies would be silenced, and that his people—that he himself—was secure. He realised just how good God is to Israel.

He makes a very interesting confession in Psalm 73; Asaph says 'I was like a beast towards you' (verse 22). An animal does not plan its day, act by its conscience, or live with eternity in view. It simply lives by instinct. Unlike man, created by God to stand on two legs and look upwards, an animal walks on four legs and looks downwards, simply reacting instinctively to situations it comes across moment by moment.

Asaph says, 'I was like that. But in the sanctuary I remembered that I was in the presence of eternity. I remembered that there is a covenant love that does not let me go, that holds me by my right hand.' Even when Asaph was drifting away from God, when the things of God were becoming eclipsed by the darkness of Asaph's intellect to the point that he wondered if it was worth continuing the disciplines of faith at all, God was holding him fast. All the time God was holding him. He never moved. He remained the same faithful covenant God that he always was.

There were circumstances in Asaph's life which he made more difficult for himself. Christians do that sometimes. I have seen many good Christian people respond to difficult situations in entirely the wrong way. It is sometimes not possible for you to make your situation better, but it is certainly possible to make it worse. You can multiply the difficulty by your reaction to it and by your own sinful response.

Yet even when we do that, God keeps holding on to us, and he is determined not to let us go. He has loved us with an everlasting love. We come to him with new sins, or perhaps confessing old sins again; and again he simply points us to the 'fountain filled with blood drawn from Immanuel's veins'. He says 'Wash and be clean.' He says that there is 'no condemnation for those who are in Christ Jesus' (*Rom.* 8:1). The blood is shed, the cross has done its work, the atonement is complete. Even when I have to confess my own unfaithfulness, I rejoice in God's absolute faithfulness.

Asaph thought he had no security—his feet had almost slipped. Yet God was holding on to him. It's so easy to forget that in the world—you need to go into the sanctuary to understand it. Hear Asaph's confession:

Whom have I in heaven but you? And there is nothing on earth that I desire besides you. My flesh and my heart may fail, but God is the strength of my heart and my portion for ever (*Psa.* 73:25-6).

This is the only place of security and safety: 'Whom have I but you?'

Dear Christian, is it not the case that after all you have been through, and in all you may be going through now, the Saviour is all the more precious to you because of his faithfulness and the abundance of his mercy? Haven't you learned that your heart will fail, but God is your heart's everlasting portion? The sanctuary will teach you that. In Jesus, you come into the presence of God; in his word, his voice speaks to your soul; by his Spirit, your understanding is opened; through his grace you see further than you can see with your reason. And one of the things you see is that his love is strong, and it lasts forever.

Asaph understood not only that God was keeping him safe in life; he was also reminded that there is an 'afterward': 'You guide me with your counsel, and *afterwards* you will receive me to glory' (*Psa.* 73:24). Life is a strange thing; we instinctively think that *here* is forever. But here is not forever. Here is just a world of shadows. It is little wonder the Christian life can sometimes be a conundrum, and the believer can be a mystery to himself. You are a child of eternity living in time. It is easy to be caught up in the things of time, and to forget the things of eternity.

That is why you need God's sanctuary, so that faith will understand. You must live by faith. So when you come into God's presence on God's day around God's word to listen to God's voice, you will understand that there is an 'afterwards' to it all. There are things that are ordinarily invisible and eternal, which you will see only if you gaze at them through the lenses of the word of God. As you do, then you will get strength and grace and courage to go out into the world of time. There you must live and work, and there you do your labour for the Lord. There you will meet the difficulties that this wilderness world will throw up. But in the sanctuary you will be reminded that there is an 'afterwards' and that afterwards will be glory.

Isn't that interesting? The purpose of the sanctuary was to reveal God's glory. Moses recorded in Exodus 40:34 that 'the glory of the LORD filled the tabernacle.' When the Ark of the Covenant was placed in the Holy Place of God's temple in Jerusalem, 'the glory of the LORD filled the house of the LORD' (*1 Kings* 8:11). When Jesus 'tabernacled' among us, as the minister of the true sanctuary (*Heb.* 8:2), it was his glory that John saw (*John* 1:14). The Spirit who indwells us as his temple is a glory-Spirit:

Now the Lord is the Spirit, and where the Spirit of the Lord is, there is freedom. And we all, with unveiled face, beholding the glory of the Lord, are being transformed into the same image from one degree of glory to another. For this comes from the Lord who is the Spirit (*2 Cor.* 3:17-18).

So it is interesting that Asaph should say that his presence in the sanctuary should remind him that afterwards all will be glory. When John saw into the throne-room of heaven, he said that 'the sanctuary was filled with smoke from the glory of God' (*Rev.* 15:8). Yet at the same time he saw that in heaven, the new Jerusalem, there was no temple, because Jesus is the temple of heaven, and no sun or moon, for Jesus is the light of heaven (*Rev.* 21:22-23). The glory of heaven sends a beam through the word into the believer's soul, which enables him to bear the present with the promise of 'afterwards'.

Faith and understanding

So what is the conclusion for Asaph? He says 'It is good for me to draw near to God.' Richard Sibbes comments:

> The sanctified spirit of a holy man, he looks not to the stream of the times, what be the currents, and opinions, and courses of rising to preferment, of getting riches, of attaining to an imaginary present happiness here; but he hath other thoughts, he hath another judgment of things, and therefore goes contrary to the world's course ... he fetcheth the rule of his life from the experimental goodness he had found by a contrary course to the world. Let the world take what course they will, 'it is good for me to draw near to God.'[8]

---

[8] Sibbes, *Works*, vol. 7, pp. 84-5.

And it will be good for you too to draw near to God. Keep looking by faith at what your eye cannot see. Let God open your eyes to the invisible glories that belong to the covenant of his grace: he is good to his people, better than they have even begun to imagine. One day we will step out of time and into eternity; but here, in time, we may step into eternity, and draw near to God in his holy place, in order that we might bear witness to his works as we live in a world of sin and sinners.

Will you live by faith in what God has spoken in his word?

When I tried to understand this,
　　it was all too hard for me
Till I came into God's temple—
　　then I saw their destiny;
For on slippery ground you place them,
　　and destroy them utterly.

How they're shattered in a moment,
　　swept away by sudden fear!
As a dream when one awakens,
　　so, O Lord, when you appear,
You will mock their aspirations,
　　and their hopes will disappear.

When my spirit was embittered
　　and my heart with grief brought low,
Like a beast I was before you—
　　dull, in understanding slow.
Yet, O Lord, you hold my right hand;
　　with you I will always go.

To your glory you will bring me
    with your counsel as my guide.
I have none but you in heaven;
    all on earth I lay aside.
Flesh and heart may fail, but ever
    God my portion will abide.

Those far off from you will perish;
    you give them their due reward.
As for me, it is a blessing
    to be near the Sovereign LORD.
I have made my God my refuge;
    all your deeds I will record.

          (Psalm 73:16-28, *Sing Psalms* version)

The Banner of Truth Trust originated in 1957 in London. The founders believed that much of the best literature of historic Christianity had been allowed to fall into oblivion and that, under God, its recovery could well lead not only to a strengthening of the church, but to true revival.

Inter-denominational in vision, this publishing work is now international, and our lists include a number of contemporary authors along with classics from the past. The translation of these books into many languages is encouraged.

A monthly magazine, *The Banner of Truth*, is also published. More information about this and all our publications can be found on our website or supplied by either of the offices below.

THE BANNER OF TRUTH TRUST

3 Murrayfield Road
Edinburgh, EH12 6EL
UK

PO Box 621, Carlisle,
Pennsylvania 17013,
USA

www.banneroftruth.org